WORLD WITHOUT FINISHING

T0079894

Books by Peter Cooley

The Company of Strangers
The Room Where Summer Ends
Nightseasons
The Van Gogh Notebook
The Astonished Hours
Sacred Conversations
A Place Made of Starlight
Divine Margins
Night Bus to the Afterlife

WORLD WITHOUT FINISHING

PETER COOLEY

Carnegie Mellon University Press
Pittsburgh 2018

Acknowledgments

Certain of these poems, or version of these poems, have appeared in the following magazines, and the author is grateful to the editors for permission to reprint.

Agni: "Villanelle"; *Bennington Review*: "Poem for Early Morning, Not an Aubade," "Spirit Dog Etc"; *Christian Century*: "Aubade," "Rembrandt, *Titus Van Rijn Possibly As St. Francis of Assisi*," "Rodin, *The Cathedral* ('And When the Hands')"; *Chronicles: A Magazine of American Culture*: "Poem for Early Morning Not an Aubade"; *Conte*: "Michelangelo, *Pietà*"; *Colorado Review*: "The Light from Certain Houses"; *Crazy Horse*: "Incarnation"; *Denver Quarterly*: "Psalm"; *The Hampden-Sydney Poetry Review*: "Open Hand, Open Wings"; *Hotel Amerika*: "Dead Cat Log Jam"; *The Hudson Review*: "The Immortality Factor"; *Image*: "The Holy Fool Meets Himself on One of His Highways"; *Louisiana Cultural Vistas*: "Carville Leper Colony, Carville, Louisiana, the Cemetery"; *Missouri Review*: "Eschatologies," "The Lesson of the Stars Is Perishing," "The Aviary," "Morning Prayer"; *The New Yorker*: "Company of the Motel Room"; *Notre Dame Review*: "A Premature Afterlife," "Mayfly Colloquy"; *Oxford American*: "BTW"; *Plume*: "Past the Sexual Rapture Which Isn't Sex," "Rodin, *The Cathedral* ('Summer Is Here')," "Presentiments," "Madrigal," "The Question," "Company of the Morning"; *Poetry Daily*: "Poem for Early Morning, Not an Aubade"; *Poets.org* (*Poem-a-Day*): "Another of the Happiness Poems"; *Prairie Schooner*: "Is This All the Gods Ask of Us"; *Sewanee Review*: "Premonition Update"; *Sewanee Theological Review*: "Star-Bottom Boat"; *Southern Review*: "Letter to Summer from the Other Side"; *Superstition Review*: "Rembrandt, *The Adoration of the Shepherds*"

The author is grateful to both the state of Louisiana for an Atlas Grant and to the Dean's and Provost's Offices of Tulane University for COR and Lurcy grants which permitted travel projects and time for the completion of these poems. Thanks is due to the English Department of Tulane University for additional financial and emotional support.

Thanks to the Faulkner Society of New Orleans for the Marble Faun Prize for Poetry; to the Louisiana Endowment for the Humanities; and to the Governor's Office, State of Louisiana, for the Poet Laureateship.

Thanks, too, to the Perkers, Carolyn Hembre, Kay Murphy, Brad Richard, Andy Young, Melissa Dickey, Andy Stallings, Katie Balma and Rodney Jones for their criticism and support.

Particular thanks are due to Jacki Cooley, Nicole Cooley, Josh Cooley and Alissa Cooley Rowan for their love, patience and sagacity.

Book design: Bronwyn Kuehler

to the God of gods

CONTENTS

ONE

TWO

Three

Four

ONE

WORLD WITHOUT FINISHING

At the end of *The Family of Man*
the last photograph, a boy and girl,

probably siblings, five and three maybe,
pose, backs to us as they enter a forest

in soft focus, the leaves silver, shivering
toward expectations beyond the scope of dawn.

Beneath it: *A world to be born under their footsteps—*
Saint-John Perse. Reader, I wish I could speak to you

without such illustration of what occurs to me
at dawn now, in my seventies, but this one image

is what I turn to, stuporous and half-awake,
my aching hand about my coffee cup assurance

the body I am carrying is a gift,
one I will give back after the last days.

That we live again is certain, that our death
is always imminent: this is the breath I draw

of faith recurrent as the sun now dappling
my back window, dappling my front at dusk.

The children walk off, they are any one of us
come back; they walk toward their death.

Immortal, you and I, soon to be born,
rush out to enter them again.

AUBADE

Sometimes, certain mornings, we are born again,
our feet traveling the floor new feet, new floor,
our window watching us cat-stretching, new

to see our yard staring, blossoming,
those flowers we newly planted yesterday
more wide-eyed than when we put them to bed.

We've never seen such hue regard the sky,
every impatiens plant's uplifted head
jubilant, defiant, red, on red, on red.

After such streaming light come to our hands
like stigmata to the saints, we shower and wait,
the old terror, our familiar, on its way—

the shaving or the make-up mirrors will hold
our bones a death mask fits, then mirror back our yards—
nothing the same color, nothing, sun's every glance.

PASTORAL

Our unknown gods are always here with us
investing shadows on the street with shape,
the cracks in the horizon with their shine,
our speech with their songs beyond mortal hearing.

We step into their darkness, our sure step
dissolving as we walk. This is the underlife,
the Lethe running straight through every choice.
We're being broken as we walk, each hour

not ours but theirs, each step their wish foretold.
Today is glorious. My face sunshine,
its features some known god's lineaments.
I am Jove, heroes I have tried to be

in imitation of epics I've read.
Write it all down, the unknowns keep repeating,
the gods so certain of its perishing,
gods assured of immortality,

jealous, enraged that they are one of us
only by trickery. And shadowless.

Morning Prayer

Let me love less, l told the mockingbird,
the first sound I heard, waking to its thrum
down the middle of the dawn, ascent and shining
portending nightfall, the panoply of stars—

let me give up old forms these words are taking.
There, I'm walking
naked, maybe, maybe wearing wind?
It's cold, I know, it's lonely.
Where are my old friends,
the homilies I learned in Sunday School?

No, it's never walking,
                              always flying.
I've given up even you, Love, climbing
these stairs I'm traveling only on my knees,
the sky a map for continents unknown,
the sky close to the bone, always new skin.

RODIN, *THE CATHEDRAL*

And when the hands give up their prayers to air—
hands which lie open, waiting for evening—
morning will answer, whether we hear or not.

Always there are these correspondences—
many nights, desperate, I have asked for sleep.
There wasn't much more I could bargain for.

Like a small child, I promised to be good.
The gods understood. Yes, impossible.
Eons they'd asked humankind for bodies

they might dwell in, bodies flawed and mortal.
They knew hunger for ineluctables.
Last night, I asked to be reborn today.

Well, here I am. And how am I doing,
you, gods, who yesterday inspired me
to sit down and, against my will, to write?

THE IMMORTALITY FACTOR

Moon-pulsing-wide the light inside the sky
always before me, mornings when I pray.

But then a treasure trove of seas comes in,
the low, the high, the tidelines watching me,

their gold detritus dawn, night-deconstructed.
And next, incessant push and pull of water music

such as these lines are trying to reconstruct.
I stoop to spell the waters for seashells,

here in my room, a word for every shell,
my certain trophies of success, of failure.

Meanwhile, the gods, their home this morning
my blue horizon asunder with lightning,

maintain their kind of watch, wild jealousy
disguised in their performance as these clouds

precipitously shape-shifting to swirl,
fall, swirl, as if the rhythm of a poem.

They'd give up immortality for one,
just one word, one poem. They are murderous,

these gods. Lear said, *They kill us for their sport.*
Shakespeare was wrong. They'd kill us for one line.

MICHELANGELO, *PIETÀ*

Beyond the stars inside noon, light you see
by teaching yourself to adopt blindness,
another light waits to be taken on,
the light inside invisibilities.
That's why I write these lines, to enter in.

Beginning, I am there. It's that simple.
The map I'm smashing inside Mary's face
because I've wanted to assemble it
so I could reassemble who I am
when I return here in my mind—that map

many a morning brings me here to pray,
by which I mean inscribing what I hear
inside these traceries of suffering stone.
Many a moment I have entered grace
such as the stars, invisible, must know—

they never thought they'd be reflecting me.

Is This All the Gods Ask of Us

that we admit someday we all will die?
We offer them that trifle every day.

But every morning, stars against my face
until they're blinded by the sun at noon,

I go out, half my belief dumb faith,
my eyes half-lidded on invisibles

but focused on my dog, scattershot mutt.
He leads this blind man on his morning walk.

I follow his tail. I follow the red hole
allowing him his random defecations.

Never the morning I thought I might see
but only this competing paradise,

these gold rivets the skyline's fastened with,
these silver-embossed footsteps where I dance,

these ever-changing weathers of my words
nectar to me, honeys and ambrosias.

My dog has never thought about his death.
This is why, long after I am gone,

his progeny, never aspiring to soul,
will lead some other fool down other streets,

who tells himself, that fool, imperishings
lie either side, sheer beauty of the world.

A world like the New Orleans' live oaks,
a sheen on leaves we've never seen before!

Since we have eyes to time our stay on earth,
and feet to claim our place, our vanishings.

Since You Asked

What gods? Why, those I make up as I go
to pave the way, the abyss splitting my floor,
a sky my ceiling opens out of habit,

the fuck-alongs of Greece and Rome—
gods in human form!—the fire in all things
the ancients bring to earth so they can rise.

These are the deities of multiplicity.
Nothing I've said can interdict our way
with one god. Just admit it: you choose one.

Without the shadow walking by my side
never cast by me, I could not continue.
That shadow's always there, I turn, turn back.

Without His shadow, how could I know light,
the light that dims the sun and never dims,
the one from the beginning of the world?

CLAIR DE LUNE

Adjacent sparrow, I will call you god
until another moment comes to wake me up.
You're just the first of my contingencies.

I'm fastening myself to your prayer wheel.
I'm bound up in your gray circumferences,
this spinning-dizzy my own place on earth.

Sparrow, I'm going to leave you soon.
Another god has flown in, silver wings
tucked into her round corners, the moon standing

in watch now I'm outside. She'll disappear
moments from now. But I can claim she's here,
ancient goddess where I can fix my eye.

Then there will be some others' grandchildren.
Sparrow, you know the gods choose us, don't you?
I'm just these few lines waiting for new shapes.

Transfiguration, send me someone new.

INCARNATION

For me, the frog on the cusp of a ditch,
accidentally riven by the storm last night,
the back of my backyard—this is my divine—

snatched in the comer of my eye, while I attend
to the serious business of raking up.
The miraculous no coincidence.

My frog, he's accompanied by a quick worm
loosening dirt he scoops up, advancing—
a bevy of worms, the hue of human flesh,

of my fingers I long to push among the quickenings . . .
I don't dare to interfere. Gods, we love each other.
You can't descend the old ways, can you?

PRESENTIMENTS

Such as the sun might present—out of sight—

I need to see the Unseen Face again,
the one I can imagine, piece by piece.
I'm talking about divinity, of course.

I need to enter where I've never been.

What else is new, my soul asked from the tree
where it had taken on the mockingbird
breaking the dawn down, splinters I could hear,
notes too high, too low, ordinary days.

The face is there, open your hand right now,
the bird kept singing me, in broken notes,
and then it made me speak, in these poor words:

the face returns my stare, oh, just reflection,
stars, stars I find along my street each day,

clogged, festering across the gutter trap.

THE LESSON OF THE STARS IS PERISHING

I've held myself against each bartered face
I've found in starlight strewn across the grass,
the mirror of the constellations there
cracked by expectation of reflection.

And when—but let me talk about the sun.
Nothing else is like imagining
the radiance the sun permits, insists.
So present no one else can wear my face,
not even me beyond the minutes it presents,
changing me while I speak, a single tree
called out of a shadow we could forget.
I mean the magnolia in my yard.
I mean my own shadow, calling me back.

Noontime moving through the trees. Weather-watch,
who am I each morning that I dare ask?

THE QUESTION

There is another light beyond the sun,
the light you have to find out for yourself.
I've seen the face of Christ in morning light
like the ancients, like children or sages.
But it's the light inside the stars at noon—
seeing it for years—that still astonishes.

I show my visions to the evening trees,
the trees inside this room, writing my lines,
the morning trees which teach me how to pray.
Sometimes the silence of eternity,
my touchstone, just too much astonishes.

How much do you remember, Reader,
from the other side, the ripe eternity
you saw this morning in the waking sun?
This is what Christ wanted me to ask you . . .

Two

AUBADE

When I cry I become another man.
I join Achilles, sulking in his tent,
Hamlet before his father's ghost and Lear
undoing his last button, then another last—

I go out, the elements conspiring
to help me find my birthplace among them,
the rain watching, the sun among the clouds
appearing only to disappear, appear—

Even these dawn birds—I always cry first light—
they, too, have their answering, in chorus.
If only I bore their monotonies! My notes?
Improvisations always underfoot,

the sky gives off, heaven, dying, rising—
I wouldn't find myself then among these leaves.
It's morning, my bower magnolia's waxen one
dividing the sky as it falls, through the sun—

if I could sing one corresponding note—
just one bar—no, I'd want a symphony—
just one.
            The sky clears, then re-forms again.
It's time I went in, I'll be someone new

I talked myself into when the sky fell—

Morning Walk: Alternate Afterlife

I'll need to find some second paradise
when I am dead, reborn, starving to come back
with hunger, thirst for a return to earth—
return to this morning, gold on everything.

You see, I take this radiance for premonition,
the beauty of the trees' transfiguration
accompaniment to the sky's melodies
I've never heard but I assume are waiting,

scores of heavenly musics answering
themselves, arrivals in the steps of intervals.
But as the block-on-block, my neighborhood
of the familiar houses' faces, unfold before me

nothing is anything but new! And I need words,
new syllables walking together as they run
to answer. That kind of gold, that silver.

Psalm

Sooner than heaven, the light across the floor,
nimbus on nimbus to the angels there

ascending and descending, never asked for,
the dust motes ladder of the unseen seen.

Sooner than music coming through the trees
where there are no branches, no roots but stars,

that prelude to all grace notes, clear and mute.
Sooner the blue, legend the reach of clouds.

Sooner the statue in the morning park
commemoration of the wind in flesh.

Sooner that statue's fracture, multiple
effigies for formlessness and namelessness.

Sooner the future in my morning fist:
the sun's descent last night its sure ascent.
Illuminations. Should I open my hand.

WINDOW ZUIHITSU

1. Windows! Brothers I never had. Sisters sane, clear, unlike my mad, abusive sister, dead.

2. *Éblouissant.* French words I like to taste. *Étincelle Malgré.* I like them all, stippled on the tongue.

3. Always here, windows, even invisible, standing beside me, walking, running, windows of the levee road. Windows eyes of the soul? Who is seeing whom?

4. Blake said: *cleanse the panes of perception.* Door-windows. Break down every door and set clear vision there. Wings, then. Wind and wings.

5. Blake went to the door naked. Who looked on him, genius he was? Mike, who knows more about Blake than I, said he did this only once. Maybe even I could do it once.

6. Once is enough for everything. I have seen, though, down my God-spaces again and again, which can open almost anywhere. Walking the levee. Windows but transparent. My window, translucent.

7. God always watching us, as they teach in Sunday School. The soul a window, always watching God.

8. Prose is a clear river, poetry a muddied lake, afraid of too much clarity.

9. To be scene and to see, the moment and its passing into moments. And then a life is over, like the mayfly's day.

10. Travel is only new language. Shall I go to Russia, just because I'm reading *The Brothers K*? Sometimes I know just how dumb I am.

11. But I won't be learning Russian or even trying. Czech was a bust. I couldn't understand a word they spoke. It sounded like phlegm, gold phlegm but nevertheless phlegm they spit at me.

12. Why can't I just travel around my room—like Dickinson? But she had a bigger room than I do, in every way.

13. I'd like the glass house they talk about in *The Duchess of Malfi*. All windows, all ready for any weather, rain or scorch, a greenhouse, a terrarium, a room we can walk around in, the sun and I, walk and talk.

Open Hand, Open Wings

We have to write our poems from paradise—
the first line takes us—to the other side—
quickly the little blue boat in your hand
sails through the archipelagoes, the isles—

new gods inhabit daily if we choose.

Out of the ordinaries of your day,
the disrepairs, the dust along your sleeve,
gold if you ask it, the cracked, the fracturing,
down every step the dragonflies present—

your feet dancing, caught in the undertow
their wings are washing up in your backyard.
Out of these, I say, our eyes are opened,
laying down lines across the broken world.

We have survived our lives. We're twice alive.

Rodin, *The Prodigal Son*

I
Now in the only day that I can know
I'll find my way to heaven when I speak.
Not your kind of supernals, mine are here,
just counting minutes as the sky comes down,
my singular deliverance, language.

II
Sometimes when I can't sleep, I see this stance:
on his knees, head thrown back, arms stretching out
as if forgiveness were the upper air
just out of reach but to appear to him
by asking the unseen gods, just asking.

His body exposed, open to attack,
the muscles of the unseen, let me sleep—

COMPANY OF THE MORNING

Enter us in the ledger of the stars
I said to the horsefly stuck against the glass,
battering his last on mud-pocked panes
I should have washed last week
with tears. I'm crying now. He's crying.

Together we can see through to our star,
the fabricated-from-dust polestar,
my fear of blazing there, his of eternity.

We know we have this moment here together,
fly's till his end, a few seconds from now,
mine unknown, extinguishment some second sight
unpeeling the constellations beyond this one.

Let's try to be one lamenting, winging minute,
split-second-now this sun looking after me
decades. Oh, no, he's gone. I'm alone, my always.

HOLY SATURDAY

Where will I be when I confront the dark
the stars have lived in for millennia?

I'm no ascetic, I love what I call
earthly paradise, this vegetable stand
beside the road. I love to buy, devour
seconds after purchase, peach juice on my chin,

my sticky fingers unfit for anything
except delicious licentiousness,
licking them clean, tonguing sweetness, myself.

But to keep hungry I need this unwavering
certain doubt I find in stars at noon,
the numinous l think I'm making up
some days. And other days I count on, countless.

ESCHATOLOGIES

The corner of my room I call my gods
greets me mornings, speechless.
It wants to be desired for its flesh
it doesn't have, its words, all gray dumb show,
its hunger for transcendence I call mine.

What I like is a journey without map,
a piece of the sky transposed on the floor
into stained glass of a cathedral,
the flight of a dozen dragonflies
I rename angels heralding, heralding.

Whatever was before invisible
this next second is form in multitudes.
Why, I've flown countless corners just on words
I never knew I'd read until I spread them, wide,
lifting the sky under my feet. Always the same sky, twice.

The Holy Fool Meets Himself on One of His Highways

Down the long road leading me back to me
I saw my holy friends, I called hello.
This is not allegory, mind me well.
I do not speak in tongues or prophecy.
I talk in the plain speech of poetry,
which is to say, the morning gives me stars,
leftover nights from which to fabricate
a path such as the first inhabitants
on earth, our ancestors, apes standing up,
could look to and by finding direction,
name Cassiopeia, the Pleiades.

Hereafter followed the great voyages,
the three who blindly followed light to light
they came to call God in mythologies,
the rounding of the Cape and continents
speaking, given languages of their own.

I said this poem is only about me:
when I came to believe, I was a speck
the light came to, I had my place on earth.
It didn't matter how tiny I am,
how short my stay—being here, I always was,
I will be, am, matter's never destroyed.
I'm the first man, the last man, shouting this.

BASTARD GHAZAL: MARY CASSATT, *LADY AT THE TEA TABLE*

"A woman should be beautiful—or dead,"
my lover swore, turning me over. Now I'm dead.

He said he liked me ass-up in our bed.
But in this poem, I'm looking past him, dead.

Ekphrasis has me three times live, and read
for a millennia, while Miss Cassatt is dead.

She was Mary-quite-contrary-never-wed,
who painted me in coffin-blue so dead-

ly I could have vanished, all blue dust instead
of immortality I'm garnering now dead.
My daughter sent this portrait back. She said,
"Mama, your nose sticks up, a tomb erected for the dead."

We never paid Cassatt. I've heard she led
a nun's life once Ramrod Degas was dead.

Her thighs sweated for him. But wouldn't go to bed.
Beside me, her *Self-Portrait* gawks at us naked, dead.

Midnights, his *Self-Portrait* comes: I give him head.
Or he goes down on me. Now we're all—but Peter Cooley—dead.

SONG

Suture me into a small eternity,
Lord, make me a pupal sack of startled light,

enough cocoon to hatch stars' butterflies,
their wings spread over endlessness confined.

Their wingspread over the endlessness, its edge?

Break me in pieces, numberless, my dust
inconsequential filaments on fire

only because speaking lights their path,
their circling, a new planet, darkening.

A new planet widening the dark?

When I can lose myself entirely, I am found
here in this morning I've awakened to

just now, black rain, a single bird
tremolo in the darkness you have seen

and made, one moment in the eternities
you remake, you return to, as I speak

you're made from, out of your time, the other side.

A Premature Afterlife

What kind of heaven will you find on Mars?
I've discovered mine planting my feet
on sepia revealing paradise
the morning walk can sketch, the evening walk,
down the same street encircling my house,
enclosure of the dance never the same.

I like the limits of a sky on fire
western nights, the frontier openings
mornings in winter, the distances sewn black
so threads of light can weave a tapestry,
one thread enough for me to hang a wall,
tomorrow's tomorrow falling, to rise again.

My eyes blinded to see, to see, blinded,
what sort of afterlife can outshine this?

THREE

POEM FOR EARLY MORNING, NOT AN AUBADE

Wonderfully established, the sun across my plate,
the white plate of morning strewn with stars
I had forbidden to go home last night,

and wonderfully next their act, the sun and stars,
wonderfully together how they mate
the way the plate has waited for, turning its pears,

its peaches to this moment, longing, longing,
the moon, a sure essential instrument,
singing along as an accompaniment;

yet coming to this instant in my life again
I'm starving for this moment to be mine,
possible even, since always, I'm outside

transcribing the sky as it disarms the earth,
celestial fractures, dismemberments,
everywhere heaven, lightning in my hands—

Another of the Happiness Poems

It's not that we're not dying.
Everything is dying.
We hear these rumors of the planet's end
none of us will be around to watch.

It's not that we're not ugly.
We're ugly.
Look at your feet, now that your shoes are off.
You could be a duck,

no, duck-billed platypus,
your feet distraction from your ugly nose.
It's not that we're not traveling,
we're traveling.

But it's not the broadback Mediterranean
carrying us against the world's current.
It's the imagined sea, imagined street,
the winged breakers, the waters we confuse with sky

willingly, so someone out there asks
are you flying or swimming?
That someone envies mortal happiness,
like everyone the other side, the dead

who stand in watch, who would give up their bliss,
their low tide eternity, rippleless,
for one day back here, alive again with us.
They know the sea and sky I'm walking on

or swimming, flying, they know it's none of these,
this dancing-standing-still, this turning, turning,
these constant transformations of the wind
I can bring down by singing to myself,

the newborn mornings, these continuals—

Past the Sexual Rapture Which Isn't Sex

Slow rain, slow morning, no one out but me.
As I walk by them, every house a prayer
refusing to begin its opening lines.

Here, there, a light comes on in front windows
"scintillant like fallen stars or fireflies"
I'd say if I were writing poetry,
but since I'm not I'll tell you it's just God
showing up with tedious coincidence.

God's always talking to me in silence,
telling me there's music in this cold rain.
I have to put my face against its face,
thrust myself past the sexual rapture
which isn't sex but has to speak that way
since I am mortal man, mortal body.

Soul, come out now, admit this is a body.

It's wonder showing up in unrhymed lines.
It's nothing much but just a song of praise.
Who gives a flying fuck about the rain?
It's just heaven come down to talk to me.
Peter, speak, man, you know how to do this.
Start: transcribe this sky in mortal language.

VILLANELLE

When I sleep I become another man.
I have to tell myself: you're going to sea.
Then I let go, swimming beside you, woman.

I love the turn and counterturn, unplanned
our bodies undergo, floating, released.
When I sleep I become another man.

It means my body faces you or lands
in turning on an island, chin to knees.
Then I let go, swimming beside you, woman.

Or, waking in the dark, I touch your hand.
No, I won't drown. Your fingers hold me, steady.
When I sleep I become another man.

We master this by not trying, we can
together keep perfecting it, can't we?
Now I let go, swimming beside you, woman.

Each night we lie down in transformation.
Where will the hours take us wordlessly?
When I sleep I become another man.
Then I let go, swimming beside you, woman.

CARVILLE LEPER COLONY, CARVILLE, LOUISIANA, THE CEMETERY

Their gravestones stand, monotonous white waves
washed up to wash in place, and then wash back,
always maintaining anonymity.

My guide says residents could take new names
committed to the leprosarium.
But if they'd chosen to keep their birth name,
dying they would be given another one.
They could be someone else eternally.

The wind picks at the sleeve of my right arm, pulls cold
around my body. The sky knows its place,
its burden, to remind me who I am,
a man alive! A man who loves naming!

That's not much of a moral to draw from this,
is it? The white stones crest and break, break, crest.
Late afternoon. It's high tide for the dead.

And now, the waves stand still. I hear voices—
voices not the wind. They won't stop singing:
We'd trade eternity for our birth names,
for even our last names—eternity.

Mayfly Colloquy

I've carved my name in morning as it comes
and as it goes, the clouds across my eyes.
This morning I'm a child if I try—
no, when I ask, asking is everything.

Heaven, you're always closer than my hand.
I never need to reach when I'm in touch
with your presence, the light inside the light.
I open my fist. You've been waiting there.

Stunned by your presence, never the same, never,
the light becomes me, seconds, then I'm back
among the perishings, the little, little, littles.

Not everyone has seen the stars I've seen,
I tell the mayfly I'm inventing here.
No, but the trillions in a single hour

allotted to us who but live a day—
why, one of our stars outshines easily
all your constellations, he sings, dying.

BLUE WINDOW: A ZUIHITSU

1 .March 19, 2014. Today my mother's birthday. But she's been dead fourteen years. Afterlife birthdays? You need to wake up.

2. Reading Reverdy's "Le même numéro," I can't grasp a thing. Impossible. Some days I read French straight-out like it's English. Today it could be Russian, Japanese. That sky out there turning to gold, then turning away.

3. Blackwindowdawn. That sky I always have my eyes on, watching me.

4. Kimiko says think lists. My lists are things Jacki wants me to do: 1. weed the front yard; 2. buy rat poison; 3. weed the back yard; 4. call the tax man; 5. go up in the attic, set out rat poison.

5. There's always possibility. Emily's word. The docent at Emily's house telling me I was related to Emily through the Higgenson line. I wanted to throw my hat into flames—where there was no fire. Out at her grave, "Called Back," those words cut in the stone. Freezing blue refusing-to-be-spring April. Where there's no proof of the bloodline, why I can just make one, who's to stop me?

6. I watched a rat die. But that was in the garage, not the attic. His choking shook his whole body, like he was dancing. I was gagging, I wanted to puke. Then I had to shovel him up and bury him behind the garage.

7. It was too late. Mother couldn't talk. Too much morphine. But first that phone call, "Don't call me up and bother me, Pete. I want to die." She had never talked that way to me before.

8. It's one of those clear, blue-gold days, blue shifting to gold, back again. Shape it into something.

9. TV says spring is two days away. March, a month of death. When our baby died it was St. Patrick' Day. I got back to the hospital after dropping off Nicole and Alissa at home. They were wrapping up the body like butcher meat. "Macerated," the nurse said, "the baby was macerated." Then Dr. Geary, "Even if it's stillborn, it weighs over a pound. You'll have to bury it." Then all that crying. I cried later.

10. The weeds in the backyard growing while I'm writing this. Through my study window the crab-grass and the dandelions watching me, triumphant.

11. Larkin said, "Life is disappointment. Then more disappointment." After he died, they found his stash: bottles of gin and porno mags.

12. When we got to the cemetery, we could see the gravedigger out the window, waiting for us. He had one foot on the edge of our plot he had already dug up. It was cold. The wind kept whipping through the gravestones. The hole was cavernous, big enough for a grown body. And her casket was so tiny. Then she was covered up. We had a little slab, no name. No name for this.

13. And always this inwardness, this turning in. Even in the midst of beauty, this inwardness. Blue wind beating the window gold because it contains the gold it ripped from trees. Just to get here. Cold spring. Colder just putting this down.

Mary Cassatt, *Children Playing on the Beach*

"There's Liz and me, she's the one in the hat,
I'm the one matrons call 'adorable'—
my face bent to a pail—since I'm chubby like them.

"A hundred years, we have become the sea
beyond our little bodies, black dresses, pinafores,
a frigate and two sailboats on our tides.

"We are that line where sea touches the sky,
our motion in blue wind invisible.
Together we've withstood a century:

"matrons, critics, Cassatt's dreams we'd live on
to give her name some immortality.
Each viewer—you—will trade a soul with us.

"We're all beyond count now. One hundred years."

SUBLUNARIES

I could have entered heaven through this crack,
the line along the floor I'm traversing
where, years back, they laid the tiles haphazardly,
zigzag peaks of clouds, that crookedness
you see when you lean in, are taken down.

Mornings I've stood here, in the kitchen, mute,
then begun, like a spider, my descent,
the heaven under the house a route skyward.

The way down, the way back, my certain wings.

Yesterday, returning through the cracked window
facing the bricks I had to lift, each one
stolen from the Great Wall of China
imagination raised to give me barricades,
I was content. Again, I'd taken a new way.

Unless the flight's impossible, why fly?
A new one every day, your wings aching.

Don't think these lines are about poetry.

Poem with a Happy Ending

Here's the old void, the circumstantial stance
the underground allows, my morning light
a streak against the chasm of the sky.

This is the oldest despair known to man.
I try my third wing, folded in its pleats,
the one I keep to navigate the skies

between Nirvana and Elysium
where heaven shines its brightest days like these.
My wing knows better than to test the dark

before full morning. I have but to wait.
All body now, dumb cock without a hen-house,
I've nothing to cock-a-doodle-doo about,

my roost this fixity, the window all my eye
I will allow myself. The void pivots and leans,
transcribed by sun, no form but radiance.

I'm one with it. I can fly out now.

REMBRANDT, *THE ADORATION OF THE SHEPHERDS*

"I am the one son of the family Rembrandt sees
come to name the light, call it miracle.
All I know is, we rushed out of the house,
Mother and Father pointing to some stars
after the shepherds raced across our farm
shouting Savior! All six sisters: Savior!
Yes, all the stars were bright. One flares, blinding.
Now it has come to watch above the crèche.

"Light shines, brightening, from inside this baby.
Me, I don't like little ones much, myself,
always stinking, wanting feeding, bawling.

"We're seven. I'm the youngest; that's the best.
Mother says, 'You're my baby.' I love that.
I push her away, squinch like I hate it.

"Look, I've brought my dog. She's called Saskia
after Rembrandt's wife. Bark, Saskia, growl,
jump for the crowd, here in the museum.
Bark! Don't you know we're with the immortals!"

THE LIGHT FROM CERTAIN HOUSES

Heaven enough, I said, but the door wouldn't close.
The light kept coming, impenetrable light,
the light from just before a paradise,
the light certain mornings choose to gift us
when we are waking, fractured, incomplete,
the light these hues church windows grant their saints,
or, in the street, rainbows smear after storms.

If this were music, it would break the ears.
If this were touch, it would macerate the flesh.
If this were habit, it would crave a fix.
If sex, my body would disappear in ash.

But it is only the unasked for come again,
the door a prayer will open now and then
and as I sing this—are you still here?—
begins to close. Closing, it's closed, I know.

And my own darkness illuminates its memory.

SPIRIT DOG ETC.

I'll have those days when I begin again,
come back as a mockingbird in the live oak,
the feral cat under your house at night,
the crone who lives beneath the underpass.

I'll be without this body, I'll be stars
no one has seen yet, illuminations
walking backwards, their faces turned toward you.

I'll be on fire; I'll be the moon, that hue
the flowers in your yard assume at night.

I'll be all immortality, won't I?

I won't be a Peter you recognize.
I'll be such winds as can befriend the air
walking beside us always, spirit dog.

I repeat. I'll be immortality.

It's only saying this I begin to live—

FOUR

OBITS

A hundred years from now we'll all be dead.
Meanwhile, let's be this mayfly in my room
whose whole life-span contracts into today.

What will we make from our hours before midnight?

There. I've spread the wings we kept concealed.
We're out the window, our past one second passed.
We've never seen a backyard in such light—
all the shrubs saints, and each one in a nimbus,

chancels of clouds stained glass, every tree a spire.
Now our breath lifts us, wind inside our wings,
what can our landing be, canyon, iceberg's peak?

I have to choose some sure extremity

where together we can lay our egg today,
not the same site as yesterday's—no, no,
yesterday's mother dead, oh, mother, o

In the Bestiary

All figurations of the morning stars
nothing but midnight light invisible—

why that's enough to start any day—
whatever lies beyond me mine to seize

as soon as I can write it here, right-sized.
I see you've started with The Grandiose,

Nightingale sings, his face against the glass,
the morning window where I come for words,

some streak of heaven thrown across the floor
even on a gray day, today, my starting point.

The Grandiose, as if you had a perch
with me in immortality of flesh.

You know I have only to sing one note,
all of your little poems can't compete.

I have pre-history running in my blood.
I draw the curtains. He can't bear the dark.

The bird knows he's just myself at twice remove,
and these words are just one-remove, each line.

He's just one of my devils, one of my animals.
I have multitudes. And now the poem.

Dead Cat Log Jam

If you would find your way to paradise,
you might ask of the stones how they maintain
the winding Mississippi levee road
you're running on this morning, river at your feet.

Stone, road, manic motion of your shoes
accompanying the songs between your breath:
What else might you have prayed for but white sky
losing that color named—nameless regaining it?

The world disdains your little figurations—
comprising how it's made. And you know this.
Today will be—what?— once you have run home?
A future tense can never let you know.

The river's other side, the houses there,
the lives beyond your vision, imagining
like yours this solitude—answer you now.
Yes, we have known this river as it stalls,

found ourselves in the black depths undone,
done, undone, and our reflection the condoms,
the cow turds, the log jam of dead cats, the scum
greening everything, living oblivion

in motion toward the Gulf, fecundity—

REMBRANDT, *TITUS VAN RIJN POSSIBLY AS ST. FRANCIS OF ASSISI*

To see the soul: impossibility.
It's in the eyes, some say, but eyes can lie
unless they're rendered in this kind of light,
the candle in the eye we call the soul,
flame of a thousand thousand flickerings
which fill the face, then the whole picture plane.

Many, I suppose, could not find the soul
in these half-lidded eyes beneath a cowl.
An exercise? To imitate a saint?
Just Rembrandt striking his son in a pose
as he becomes St. Paul, other prophets?

The soul is there! Shining first in the face
then filling every inch within this frame.
The light within can be mahogany
as well as gold this picture teaches us.

We do not need teaching, we're trading souls.

EPISTLE TO GOD

Days I am stripped clean I begin again.
I am a rib of some sea anemone,
fish or crustacean, prehistoric whale
or microscopic shell around my soul
and one of them, me, come in to cleanse the shore,
the tide line only there to bear my witness.

Or I am a skull passed by a Greyhound bus
in which Peter Cooley crawled through Texas,
College Station, Texas, eye socket stare
taking him in, 1978, and those minutes resurrect.
Someday, I know, the eyes will give me clarity
of pure intention, death a kind of immaculate
finish such as the artificial keeps, no natural worth.

But to be clean, first, now I am chosen—there are the fires,
always, I am made to pass through,
to lose the waters of recognizable intent,
to drown in new Euphrates or Black Seas

then to trod the deserts the great prophets named,
secure in my intention to be clean, new wings
the air around me, new fins high waters never seen,
new breath my death, my death again, again,
a raw imagining, a mist parting as I pass through.
Master, by your intention I take on,
slough off, the unimaginable new shapes,
my startled bones flying with fixed intent,
no distance between the sky, the ground
the sky makes up to see its own reflection,

finally no separation between I and me.

TICKETS, HAVE YOUR TICKETS READY

I won't be ready when the boat takes off.
There still will be the trees I haven't named,
between the cracks the flowers in the sky,
the dolphin who swam up, head to scratch,
his eyes so paradisal in the morning light
I couldn't hear the syllables he whispered me.

Mornings when I am occupied, always
enlarging or diminishing the world,
I hear the low, black, syncopating jazz
of the boat's whistle, its first trip of the day
departing the harbor of my window.

"Imagine faster! Someone needs your place,
your pen, your paper, computer and your books.
It's all going out in the afterlife with trash,"

the clouds begin to shout, pausing while they're passing.

No, I'll stay put. I have my place to squat.
Only the gods can unseat me, working.

And when eternity comes toward, I'll book steerage.

Premonition Update

I don't think heaven will come back
until tomorrow when I see the rain

I'm watching now drawing the trees new shapes,
the too-familiar elm, magnolia,

the live oak, roots spread out like a starfish.
I'll watch that rain all day, take in its slant—

and then some morning nothing but the slant.
Today I'm greedy for transcendences,

the fractured, dark revision of my yard
might give me if the rain would only stop.

The rain won't stop. There is no end in sight
the weather lady assures us, her map black.

This is the way that heaven come to us,
resurrection always only in our hands.

Company of the Motel Room

Red shoe under the bed, black sock
nestled inside it, burn mark the size of a man's thumb
on the nightstand: what has been ended here?
Or what begun since from such origins
no long continuance could stay itself
as my long marriage testifies by its repeated passages
of middling weather. Tracery of cigarette ash
on this window sill . . . who has stood where I stand
before or after love, asking why he came here,
why this blue spruce I'm looking on, unflinchable,
resists the winds as people never can
or why this highway encircling me, alone again—
my conference done, tomorrow I go home—
drives some to lives of rich desserts, some lives
of stolen crumbs, and for me neither. Home!
I have to find a small squall there. Start one?

THE AVIARY

I'll tell you how I believe: come with me now
down starred horizons fallen in this street,
the run-over cat spills with ruby guts.

A rook awaits me. Watch. I take his wings.
I have whole days when I fly in this rook,
the street a hunting ground for all my prayers.

Mornings when I go out to take on faith
sudden descents, I swoop, land on concrete—
what am I hunting except firm affirmation

in the clogged storm drain where water reflects stars
among tree branches, imagining each root
for me, then forests' constellations?

Each uncertain resurrection I count on?

MADRIGAL

Nights as I drop off, caw-caw-cawing of this bird.
Waking, he's at my window like black rain
the same as yesterday's, monotonous,
I can't begin to imitate in words.

I guess it's Death he's trying to sing to me,
surrounding the house, a weather falling,
rising, falling, the squall everything
the almost-dying might ask for their last hours.

I'll want him when I'm blind, deaf, impotent,
grateful this dissonance answers mine,
rivals in cacophony my last breaths
shriller than his. Then I'll be gone.

But we don't choose, do we? the birds insists—
I'm reading in, of course, but he insists
on reading in. This is just a bird, a crow,
the call says, but it hangs on the trees—

the call moves down the street, faster each day.
Some days I think it has become the street
calling me. Faster every morning, evening
even faster. The call insists. But this is just a crow—

Rodin, *The Cathedral*

Summer is here, a quiet, well-lit time.
Along my street, the trees assume their light—
to each according to ability
infinitely various, changeable.

We only have so many mornings here.
Then there will be another kind of day—
maybe. Maybe, even, the trees will speak.
I know I'd like to enter their silence,
to write a poem dumb as Rodin's stone.

Now, without asking, *The Cathedral*'s here,
these hands I have too much written about.
They are this morning, numb, expressionless.
Pretense of immortality, they pass
like this cloud I am staring at right now,
even as I speak shape-shifting and now gone.

Summer can take us all in and go on—

STAR-BOTTOM BOAT,

1. You are my mapless journey on these tides
each morning expectation lifts, shoreless.

2 .Your waves crash through each other, colorless.
You shape the tints of too much longing, stalled,

3. hues calling through each other to become
each other's rainbows, arcing, vanishing.

4. Little boat, my hopes are always in the wings
greeting us, trawling dawnward as they swoop,

5. these gulls, the terns, the pelicans on fire,
every morning a different conflagration.

6. Years back I threw away my compass, broke the wheel,
disremembered longitude and latitude.

7. On my best mornings midnight falls at noon,
the black streaks releasing constellations.

8. My luck? Little boat, it knows where we're going
and gods, my dark stars, I try to count and can't.

LETTER TO SUMMER FROM THE OTHER SIDE

Summer, remember me now I am dead.
I was the eye to wonder at the sheen
you set on all things, tree and grass and cloud,

all blossomings. I took you in.
I was a child again each time you came.
And each time you had to leave, I was the wait

hurrying the autumn, the winter and the spring
to turn toward you once more, my eye on fire.
I saw your ghost crackle the fall leaves,

October, I watched your frost cross the windows,
December. I began countdown toward June.
How many mornings, January, February,

until I saw the sky in its full bloom,
the cloudlessness where I could throw my seeds—
how many nights starving to imagine,

how many moons didn't I try to count my flowers
never before pretended, to rival yours?

Previous titles in the Carnegie Mellon Poetry Series

2001

Day Moon, Jon Anderson
The Origin of Green, T. Alan Broughton
Lovers in the Used World, Gillian Conoley
Quarters, James Harms
Mastodon, 80% Complete, Jonathan Johnson
The Deepest Part of the River, Mekeel McBride
Earthly, Michael McFee
Ten Thousand Good Mornings, James Reiss
The World's Last Night, Margot Schilpp
Sex Lives of the Poor and Obscure, David Schloss
Glacier Wine, Maura Stanton
Voyages in English, Dara Wier

2002

Keeping Time, Suzanne Cleary
Astronaut, Brian Henry
What It Wasn't, Laura Kasischke
Slow Risen Among the Smoke Trees, Elizabeth Kirschner
The Finger Bone, Kevin Prufer
Among the Musk Ox People, Mary Ruefle
The Late World, Arthur Smith

2003

Trouble, Mary Baine Campbell
A Place Made of Starlight, Peter Cooley
Taking Down the Angel, Jeff Friedman
Lives of Water, John Hoppenthaler
Imitation of Life, Allison Joseph
Except for One Obscene Brushstroke, Dzvinia Orlowsky
The Mastery Impulse, Ricardo Pau-Llosa
Casino of the Sun, Jerry Williams

2004

The Women Who Loved Elvis All Their Lives, Fleda Brown
The Chronic Liar Buys a Canary, Elizabeth Edwards

Freeways and Aqueducts, James Harms
Prague Winter, Richard Katrovas
Trains in Winter, Jay Meek
Tristimania, Mary Ruefle
Venus Examines Her Breast, Maureen Seaton
Various Orbits, Thom Ward

2005
Things I Can't Tell You, Michael Dennis Browne
Bent to the Earth, Blas Manuel De Luna
Blindsight, Carol Hamilton
Fallen from a Chariot, Kevin Prufer
Needlegrass, Dennis Sampson
Laws of My Nature, Margot Schilpp
Sleeping Woman, Herbert Scott
Renovation, Jeffrey Thomson

2006
Burn the Field, Amy Beeder
The Sadness of Others, Hayan Charara
A Grammar to Waking, Nancy Eimers
Dog Star Delicatessen: New and Selected Poems 1979–2006, Mekeel McBride
Shinemaster, Michael McFee
Eastern Mountain Time, Joyce Peseroff
Dragging the Lake, Robert Thomas

2007
Trick Pear, Suzanne Cleary
So I Will Till the Ground, Gregory Djanikian
Black Threads, Jeff Friedman
Drift and Pulse, Kathleen Halme
The Playhouse Near Dark, Elizabeth Holmes
On the Vanishing of Large Creatures, Susan Hutton
One Season Behind, Sarah Rosenblatt
Indeed I Was Pleased with the World, Mary Ruefle
The Situation, John Skoyles

2008
The Grace of Necessity, Samuel Green
After West, James Harms
Anticipate the Coming Reservoir, John Hoppenthaler
Convertible Night, Flurry of Stones, Dzvinia Orlowsky
Parable Hunter, Ricardo Pau-Llosa
The Book of Sleep, Eleanor Stanford

2009
Divine Margins, Peter Cooley
Cultural Studies, Kevin A. González
Dear Apocalypse, K. A. Hays
Warhol-o-rama, Peter Oresick
Cave of the Yellow Volkswagen, Maureen Seaton
Group Portrait from Hell, David Schloss
Birdwatching in Wartime, Jeffrey Thomson

2010
The Diminishing House, Nicky Beer
A World Remembered, T. Alan Broughton
Say Sand, Daniel Coudriet
Knock Knock, Heather Hartley
In the Land We Imagined Ourselves, Jonathan Johnson
Selected Early Poems: 1958-1983, Greg Kuzma
The Other Life: Selected Poems, Herbert Scott
Admission, Jerry Williams

2011
Having a Little Talk with Capital P Poetry, Jim Daniels
Oz, Nancy Eimers
Working in Flour, Jeff Friedman
Scorpio Rising: Selected Poems, Richard Katrovas
The Politics, Benjamin Paloff
Copperhead, Rachel Richardson

2012
Now Make an Altar, Amy Beeder
Still Some Cake, James Cummins

2016

Something Sinister, Hayan Charara
The Spokes of Venus, Rebecca Morgan Frank
Adult Swim, Heather Hartley
Swastika into Lotus, Richard Katrovas
The Nomenclature of Small Things, Lynn Pedersen
Hundred-Year Wave, Rachel Richardson
Where Are We in This Story, Sarah Rosenblatt
Inside Job, John Skoyles
Suddenly It's Evening: Selected Poems, John Skoyles

2017

Disappeared, Jasmine V. Bailey
Custody of the Eyes, Kimberly Burwick
Dream of the Gone-From City, Barbara Edelman
Sometimes We're All Living in a Foreign Country, Rebecca Morgan Frank
Rowing with Wings, James Harms
Windthrow, K. A. Hays
We Were Once Here, Michael McFee
Kingdom, Joseph Millar
The Histories, Jason Whitmarsh

2018

World Without Finishing, Peter Cooley
The End of Spectacle, Virginia Konchan
Big Windows, Lauren Moseley
Immortal Village, Kathryn Rhett
Last City, Brian Sneeden
Black Sea, David Yezzi